# TRANSPORT IN MY COMMUNITY

# TRAINS

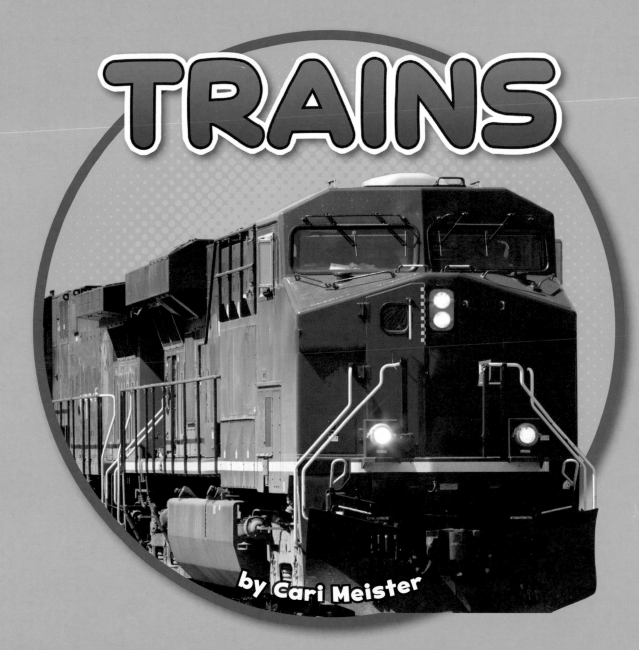

by Cari Meister

raintree

a Capstone company — publishers for children

Trains can go fast. They can carry lots of people. It can be fun to travel by train!

# Clack, clack, clack!

# WHOOOSH!

People wait for trains at stations. Some stations are big and busy. Many trains come in and out every day. Other stations are smaller and quieter.

Trains run on tracks called rails. A train runs smoothly over the metal rails. At the station, the train stops and the doors open. Some people get off and some people get on.

# Zoom! Zoom!

Underground trains travel under cities. They stop often to let people on and off.

Bullet trains are high-speed trains in
Japan. They are very fast! They can go
200 miles (322 kilometres) per hour.

Click.

Click.

Click.

Mountain trains climb up steep hills.

toothed rail

A special middle rail has grooves that look like teeth.
The toothed rail latches to the train as it climbs.
This stops the train from slipping down the tracks.

Chuk.

Chuk.

Chuk.

Cargo trains carry heavy goods, such as cars and coal. They pull up to factories to easily load and unload goods. They take goods from the factories to towns and cities all over the country.

The engine pulls the railway carriages.
The engine is big and powerful.

Railway carriages carry cargo or passengers.

Hopper wagons carry coal.

Tanker carriages carry fuel.
Trains can carry large loads quickly.
They take people and goods all over
the country!

A monorail is a type of train that runs on one rail.
People usually ride a monorail for short trips.

Some zoos have monorails. The track is up high so you can see all the animals as you travel.

A maglev train looks as if it is flying. It does not have any wheels. There are magnets on top of the train's rails. There are magnets underneath the train too.

The magnets repel each other.
This makes the train hover
above the rails and move forwards.

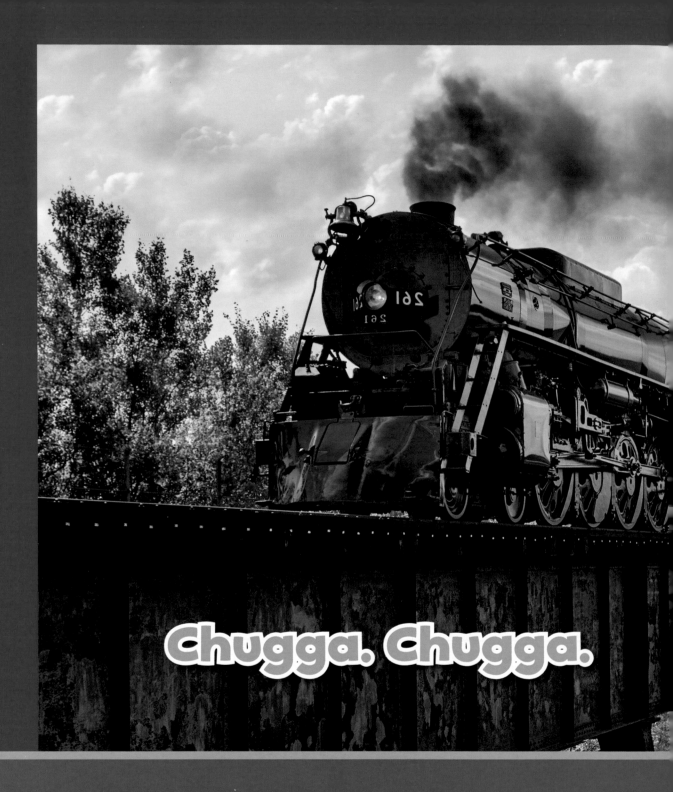

Chugga. Chugga.

Trains need power to move. The first trains were powered by steam engines.

They used fuel such as coal and wood.
They made a lot of black smoke.

In the 1940s, diesel engines replaced steam engines. Diesel trains move faster than steam trains. They are still used today. Diesel fuel burns inside the train's engine. This makes energy needed to power the motors.

Some train tracks cross roads at railway crossings. When a train is coming, lights flash to warn the cars. Sometimes a bell rings too.

# Ding. Ding. Ding.

A gate lowers to stop cars driving over the track. The cars wait while the train passes. When the train has gone, the gate lifts.

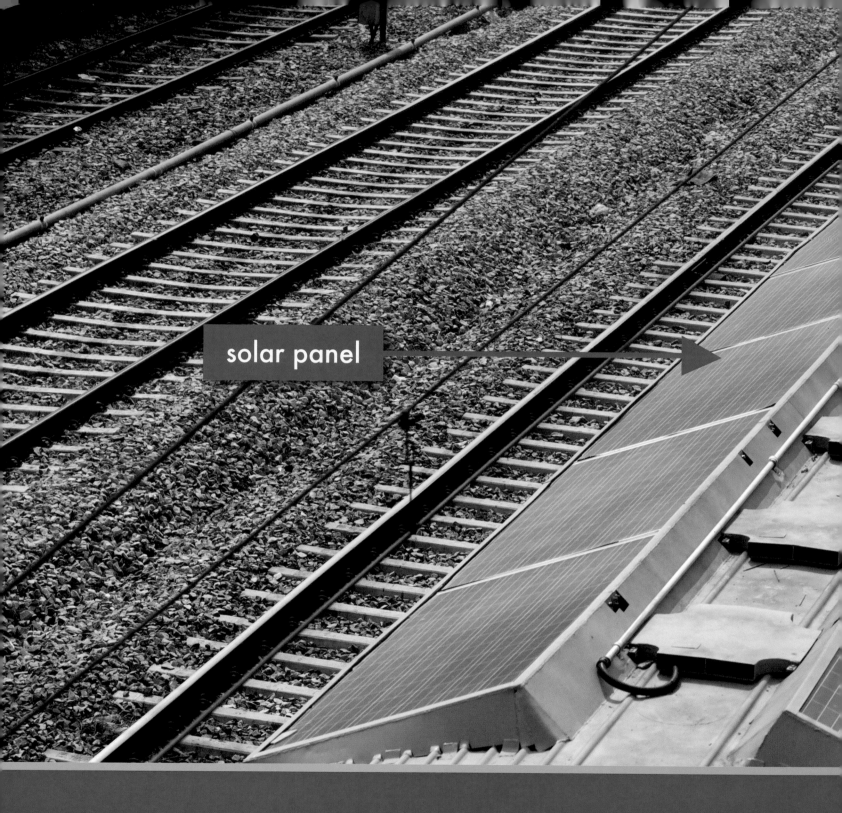

solar panel

Some trains use the Sun to move.
They have solar panels. The panels
collect the Sun's energy.

On sunny days, extra energy is stored in the train's battery. That way the train can still run when it is cloudy outside.

Trains keep changing. Today, some trains can travel through long tunnels under water!

The Channel Tunnel train takes passengers under the sea between England and France. There is an underwater tunnel train being built in India too.

# All aboard!

Millions of people travel on trains every day.
People use them to go to work, school and
on holiday.

# Where would you like to go by train?

# Timeline

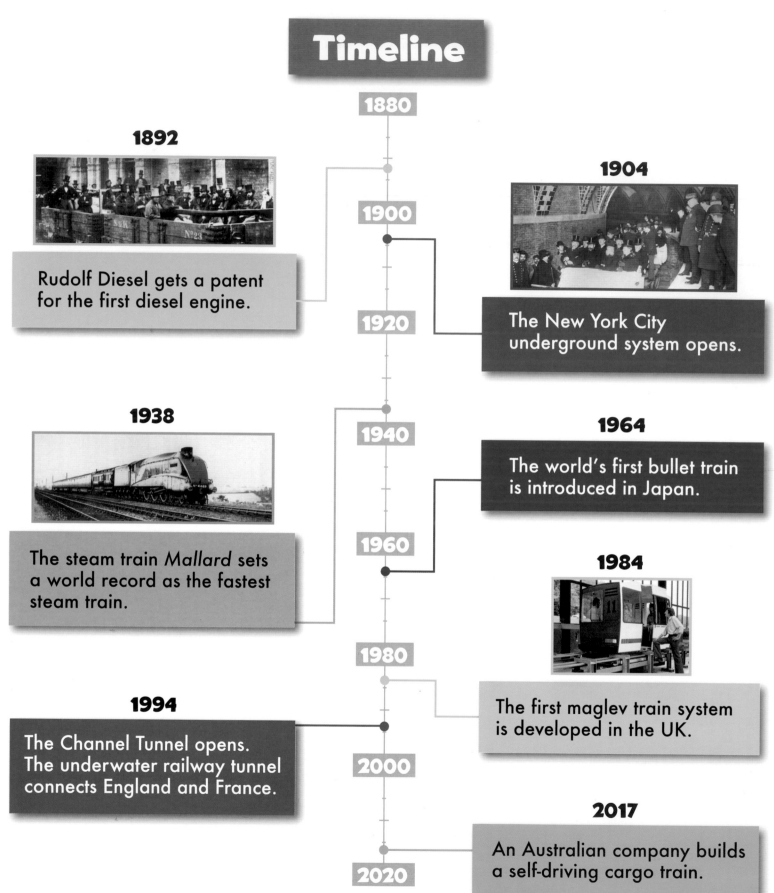

**1880**

**1892**
Rudolf Diesel gets a patent for the first diesel engine.

**1900**

**1904**
The New York City underground system opens.

**1920**

**1938**
The steam train *Mallard* sets a world record as the fastest steam train.

**1940**

**1964**
The world's first bullet train is introduced in Japan.

**1960**

**1984**
The first maglev train system is developed in the UK.

**1980**

**1994**
The Channel Tunnel opens. The underwater railway tunnel connects England and France.

**2000**

**2017**
An Australian company builds a self-driving cargo train.

**2020**

## Glossary

**cargo**  objects carried by train or other vehicle from one place to another

**diesel**  a type of fuel that burns to make power

**engine**  a machine that pulls a train

**patent**  a legal document giving someone sole rights to make or sell a product

**repel**  to push apart

**solar panel**  a flat surface that collects sunlight and turns it into power

**station**  a place where tickets for train rides are sold and where people are let on and off trains

## Find out more

*High-speed Trains* (All Aboard), Nikki Bruno Clapper (Raintree, 2015)

*My Best Books of Trains* , Richard Balkwill (Kingfisher, 2019)

*See Inside Trains* (Usborne See Inside), Emily Bone (Usborne, 2013)

## Websites

**primaryfacts.com/4645/train-facts-for-kids/**
Discover fast facts about trains, including steam trains.

**www.sciencekids.co.nz/sciencefacts/trains.html**
Check out this website for fun facts about trains.

# Index

Raintree is an imprint of Capstone Global Library Limited, a company incorporated in England and Wales having its registered office at 264 Banbury Road, Oxford, OX2 7DY – Registered company number: 6695582

www.raintree.co.uk
myorders@raintree.co.uk

Text © Capstone Global Library Limited 2020
The moral rights of the proprietor have been asserted.

Editor: Michelle Parkin
Designer: Rachel Tesch
Printed and bound in India

ISBN: 978 1 4747 7491 8 (hardback)          ISBN 978 1 4747 7492 5 (paperback)

British Library Cataloguing in Publication Data
A full catalogue record for this book is available from the British Library.

Acknowledgements
Alamy: AA World Travel Library, 15, E.Westmacott, 6 (inset); Getty Images: Arvind Yadav/Hindustan Times, 24-25, Bettmann/CORBIS, 20-21, Hulton-Deutsch Collection/CORBIS, 30 (top left), PhotoQuest, 30 (top right), Science & Society Picture Library, 30 (bottom left and bottom right); iStockphoto: BeyondImages, 23, doranjclark, 22, Grigorev_Vladimir, 12-13, halbergman, 29, haveblue, 11 (inset), ImagineGolf, 10-11, josepponsa, 9, kickstand, 2-3, Nikada, 14, pedrosala, 6-7, Stefonlinton, cover (top), 1, Yongyuan Dai, 16; Science Source: Marcello Bertinetti, 17; Shutterstock: Alf Ribeiro, 28, Aneese, cover (bottom right), Carlos Huang, cover (bottom middle), GE_4530, 12 (inset top), Geoffrey Kuchera, 18-19, Peter Gudella, cover (bottom left), Peter Stein, 8, Peter Titmuss, 5, Pieter Beens, 26-27, satephoto, 12 (inset bottom), whitelook, 4

Every effort has been made to contact copyright holders of material reproduced in this book. Any omissions will be rectified in subsequent printings if notice is given to the publisher.

All the internet addresses (URLs) given in this book were valid at the time of going to press. However, due to the dynamic nature of the internet, some addresses may have changed, or sites may have changed or ceased to exist since publication. While the author and publisher regret any inconvenience this may cause readers, no responsibility for any such changes can be accepted by either the author or the publisher.